GOD'S WONDERFUL WORLD OF LETTERS

P IS FOR PINK POLLIWOGS

Glenda Palmer and Patrick Girouard

Chariot Book
David C. Cook Publishing

D1158761

Dear Parents,

Remember how delighted your children were when they could first recite the alphabet?

Now you can help them take the next step! As you read *P Is for Pink Polliwogs* together, you can help your kids identify each letter and the sound that it makes. Soon they'll be able to find all the b's on the page and look for butterflies in the colorful illustration.

So read through *P Is for Pink Polliwogs* time and time again, and help your children discover God's wonderful world of letters.

Chariot Books™ is an imprint of David C. Cook Publishing Co.
David C. Cook Publishing Co., Elgin, Illinois 60120
David C. Cook Publishing Co., Weston, Ontario
Nova Distribution Ltd., Newton Abbot, England

P IS FOR PINK POLLIWOGS: GOD'S WONDERFUL WORLD OF LETTERS
© 1993 by Glenda Palmer for text and Patrick Girourard for illustrations

Designed by Elizabeth Thompson
First Printing, 1993
Printed in Singapore.
97 96 95 94 93 5 4 3 2 1

Palmer, Glenda.
P is for pink polliwogs : God's wonderful world of letters / by Glenda Palmer.
        p.   cm.
Summary: Presents aspects of God's creation for each letter of the alphabet, from Adam to zebras.
ISBN 0-7814-0708-7
1. Identification (religion)—Juvenile literature. 2. Alphabet—Religious aspects—Christianity—Juvenile literature. 3. Creation—Juvenile literature.
[1. Creation. 2. Christian life 3. Alphabet.] I. Title.
BV4509.5P33 1993
231.7'65—dc20
[E]   92-34715
                                                             CIP
                                                             AC

I know all about the alphabet!

A is the very first letter of the alphabet.

Alphabet begins with **A**. **A**dam begins with **A**, too. He was the first person God ever made.

God also made **B**eautiful **B**irds and fluttering **B**utterflies and **B**usy **B**ees **B**uzzing. They all begin with **B**.

A-B-C

Create. The word **C**reate begins with the letter **C**.

Create means to make something out of nothing. Only God can do that.

God created **D**arkness and called it night, and the light He called **D**ay, with a **D**.

God created **E**ve to be Adam's wife. And He made a home for them in the Garden of **E**den.

 **F** is for **F**ish, splish–splashing.

 **G** reminds me of **G**rizzly bears **G**rowling.

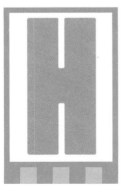

Ha, **H**a, **H**a! Laughing **H**yenas and **H**ippopotamuses begin with **H**.

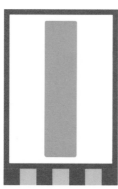

But what did God make beginning with the letter I?

I'll think about it and give it another try.

God created **J**ackrabbits,

 and **K**angaroos with built-in pockets.

L is for **L**ions and **L**ambs.
But what did God make beginning with the letter **l**?
I'll think about it and give it another try.

God created **M**ighty **M**ountains rising up, almost to the clouds.

 is for all sizes of **N**oses.

O is the first letter in **O**cean and **O**ctopus.

P is for **P**ink **P**olliwogs in **P**uddles of water. God created all the water—every drop—in this big, wide, wonderful world.

God made Quick Quails and Quiet whales that swim in the deep, wide ocean.

 And for **R**, God painted a **R**ainbow of colors—**R**ed, orange, yellow, green, blue, and purple. My favorite color is **R**ed.

God made **S**nake**S** hi**SSSSS**ing,

and all kind of **T**rees to climb
for **T**.

But what did God make beginning with the letter **I**?

I'll think about it and give it
another try.

For **U**, He created the **U**niverse, with suns and moons and stars twinkling.

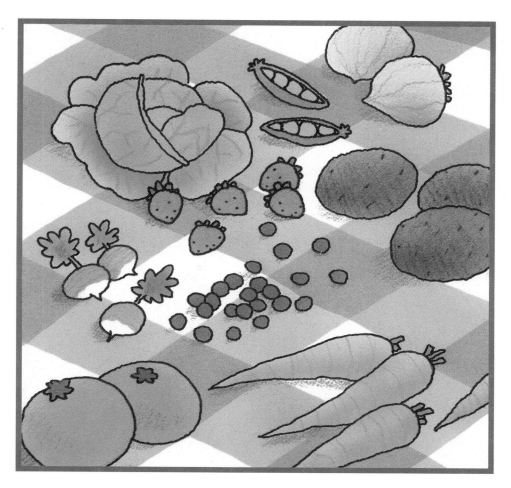

He made **V**egetables and **V**ery juicy berries for the letter **V**. What's your favorite **V**egetable?

God created this big, **W**ide, **W**onderful **W**orld!

God made something for every letter of the alphabet. For **X** He made e**X**tra e**X**tremely e**X**traordinarily ugly alligators,

for **Y**, **Y**aks and **Y**ellow
camelbacks,

and for **Z**, **Z**ebras all dressed up in black and white stripes.

But what did God make beginning with the letter **I**?

I'll think about it and give it another try.

Now **I** know! **I** am the letter **I**!

I am created by God, too. God knows all about me!

He knows my name is

_____

He knows my name begins with

God knows because He made me! And He loves me more than all the plants and all the animals and all the things He created for His big, wide, wonderful world.

I AM GOD'S SPECIAL CREATION!

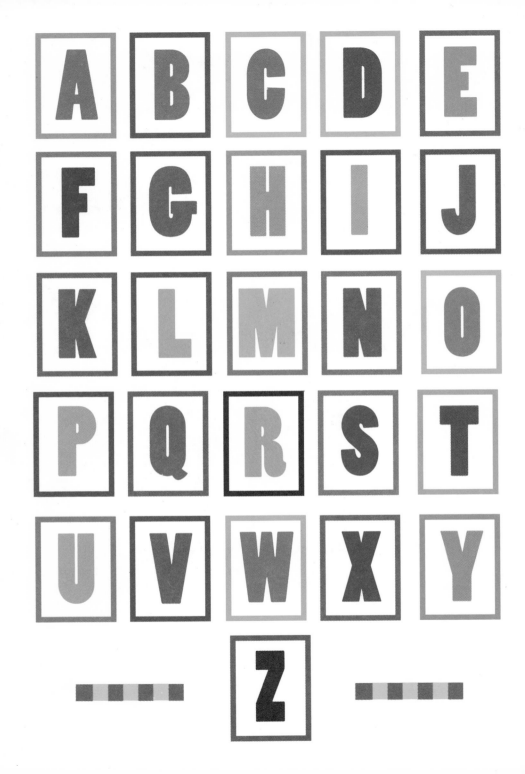